CHECKING ACCOUNT LEDGER

Name: _____

Phone: _____

onth / Year:_____ Starting balance:_____

No.	Date	Description	Debit(-)		Credit(+)		Balance

otes:_____

_____

Month / Year:_____ Starting balance:_____

No.	Date	Description	Debit(-)		Credit(+)		Balance

Notes:_____

_____

_____

onth / Year:_____ Starting balance:_____

No.	Date	Description	Debit(-)		Credit(+)		Balance

otes: _____

_____

Month / Year: _____ Starting balance: _____

No.	Date	Description	Debit(-)		Credit(+)		Balance

Notes: _____

_____

_____

Month / Year:_____ Starting balance:_____

No.	Date	Description	Debit(-)		Credit(+)		Balance

Notes:_____
_____
_____

Month / Year:_____ Starting balance:_____

No.	Date	Description	Debit(-)		Credit(+)		Balance

Notes:_____

_____

_____

onth / Year:_____ Starting balance:_____

No.	Date	Description	Debit(-)		Credit(+)		Balance

otes: _____
_____
_____

Month / Year:_____ Starting balance:_____

No.	Date	Description	Debit(-)		Credit(+)		Balance

Notes:_____

_____

_____

onth / Year:_____ Starting balance:_____

No.	Date	Description	Debit(-)		Credit(+)		Balance

otes: _____

_____

Month / Year:_____ Starting balance:_____

No.	Date	Description	Debit(-)		Credit(+)		Balance

Notes:_____

_____

_____

onth / Year:_____ Starting balance:_____

No.	Date	Description	Debit(-)		Credit(+)		Balance

otes: _____

_____

Month / Year:_____ Starting balance:_____

No.	Date	Description	Debit(-)		Credit(+)		Balance

Notes:_____

_____

_____

onth / Year:_____ Starting balance:_____

No.	Date	Description	Debit(-)		Credit(+)		Balance

otes: _____

_____

Month / Year:_____ Starting balance:_____

No.	Date	Description	Debit(-)		Credit(+)		Balance

Notes:_____

_____

_____

Month / Year:_____ Starting balance:_____

No.	Date	Description	Debit(-)		Credit(+)		Balance

Notes:_____

_____

Month / Year:_____ Starting balance:_____

No.	Date	Description	Debit(-)		Credit(+)		Balance

Notes:_____

_____

_____

No.	Date	Description	Debit(-)		Credit(+)		Balance

otes: _____
_____
_____

Month / Year:_____ Starting balance:_____

No.	Date	Description	Debit(-)		Credit(+)		Balance

Notes:_____

_____

_____

Month / Year:_____ Starting balance:_____

No.	Date	Description	Debit(-)		Credit(+)		Balance

Notes: _____

_____

Month / Year: _____ Starting balance: _____

No.	Date	Description	Debit(-)		Credit(+)		Balance

Notes: _____

_____

_____

onth / Year:_____ Starting balance:_____

No.	Date	Description	Debit(-)		Credit(+)		Balance

otes:_____

_____

Month / Year:_____ Starting balance:_____

No.	Date	Description	Debit(-)		Credit(+)		Balance

Notes:_____

_____

_____

Month / Year:_____ Starting balance:_____

No.	Date	Description	Debit(-)		Credit(+)		Balance

Notes: _____
_____
_____

Month / Year:_____ Starting balance:_____

No.	Date	Description	Debit(-)		Credit(+)		Balance

Notes:_____

_____

_____

No.	Date	Description	Debit(-)		Credit(+)		Balance

otes:_____

_____

Month / Year:_____ Starting balance:_____

No.	Date	Description	Debit(-)		Credit(+)		Balance

Notes:_____

_____

_____

Month / Year:_____ Starting balance:_____

No.	Date	Description	Debit(-)		Credit(+)		Balance

Notes:_____
_____
_____
_____

Month / Year:_____ Starting balance:_____

No.	Date	Description	Debit(-)		Credit(+)		Balance

Notes:_____
_____
_____

Month / Year: _____ Starting balance: _____

No.	Date	Description	Debit(-)		Credit(+)		Balance

Notes: _____

_____

Month / Year:_____ Starting balance:_____

No.	Date	Description	Debit(-)		Credit(+)		Balance

Notes:_____

_____

_____

onth / Year:_____ Starting balance:_____

No.	Date	Description	Debit(-)		Credit(+)		Balance

otes:_____

_____

Month / Year:_____ Starting balance:_____

No.	Date	Description	Debit(-)		Credit(+)		Balance

Notes:_____

_____

_____

onth / Year:_____ Starting balance:_____

No.	Date	Description	Debit(-)		Credit(+)		Balance

otes: _____

_____

Month / Year: _____ Starting balance: _____

No.	Date	Description	Debit(-)		Credit(+)		Balance

Notes: _____

_____

_____

Month / Year:_____ Starting balance:_____

No.	Date	Description	Debit(-)		Credit(+)		Balance

Notes:_____

_____

Month / Year:_____ Starting balance:_____

No.	Date	Description	Debit(-)		Credit(+)		Balance

Notes:_____

_____

_____

No.	Date	Description	Debit(-)		Credit(+)		Balance

otes:_____

_____

_____

Month / Year:_____ Starting balance:_____

No.	Date	Description	Debit(-)		Credit(+)		Balance

Notes:_____

_____

_____

nth / Year: _____ Starting balance: _____

No.	Date	Description	Debit(-)		Credit(+)		Balance

otes: _____

_____

Month / Year:_____ Starting balance:_____

No.	Date	Description	Debit(-)		Credit(+)		Balance

Notes:_____

_____

_____

Month / Year:_____ Starting balance:_____

No.	Date	Description	Debit(-)		Credit(+)		Balance

Notes: _____
_____

Month / Year:_____ Starting balance:_____

No.	Date	Description	Debit(-)		Credit(+)		Balance

Notes:_____

_____

_____

nth / Year:_____ Starting balance:_____

No.	Date	Description	Debit(-)		Credit(+)		Balance

otes: _____

_____

Month / Year:_____ Starting balance:_____

No.	Date	Description	Debit(-)		Credit(+)		Balance

Notes:_____

_____

_____

nth / Year:_____ Starting balance:_____

No.	Date	Description	Debit(-)		Credit(+)		Balance

otes:_____

_____

Month / Year:_____ Starting balance:_____

No.	Date	Description	Debit(-)		Credit(+)		Balance

Notes:_____

_____

_____

nth / Year:_____ Starting balance:_____

No.	Date	Description	Debit(-)		Credit(+)		Balance

otes:_____
_____

Month / Year:_____ Starting balance:_____

No.	Date	Description	Debit(-)		Credit(+)		Balance

Notes:_____

_____

_____

Month / Year:_____ Starting balance:_____

No.	Date	Description	Debit(-)		Credit(+)		Balance

Notes:_____

_____

Month / Year:_____ Starting balance:_____

No.	Date	Description	Debit(-)		Credit(+)		Balance

Notes:_____

_____

_____

nth / Year:_____ Starting balance:_____

No.	Date	Description	Debit(-)		Credit(+)		Balance

otes:_____
_____

Month / Year:_____ Starting balance:_____

No.	Date	Description	Debit(-)		Credit(+)		Balance

Notes:_____

_____

_____

Month / Year:_____ Starting balance:_____

No.	Date	Description	Debit(-)		Credit(+)		Balance

Notes:_____

_____

Month / Year:_____ Starting balance:_____

No.	Date	Description	Debit(-)		Credit(+)		Balance

Notes:_____

_____

_____

Month / Year:_____ Starting balance:_____

No.	Date	Description	Debit(-)		Credit(+)		Balance

Notes:_____
_____

Month / Year: _____ Starting balance: _____

No.	Date	Description	Debit(-)		Credit(+)		Balance

Notes: _____

_____

_____

Month / Year:_____ Starting balance:_____

No.	Date	Description	Debit(-)		Credit(+)		Balance

Notes:_____

_____

Month / Year:_____ Starting balance:_____

No.	Date	Description	Debit(-)		Credit(+)		Balance

Notes:_____

_____

_____

nth / Year:_____ Starting balance:_____

No.	Date	Description	Debit(-)		Credit(+)		Balance

otes:_____

_____

Month / Year:_____ Starting balance:_____

No.	Date	Description	Debit(-)		Credit(+)		Balance

Notes:_____

_____

_____

Month / Year:_____ Starting balance:_____

No.	Date	Description	Debit(-)		Credit(+)		Balance

Notes:_____

_____

Month / Year: _____ Starting balance: _____

No.	Date	Description	Debit(-)		Credit(+)		Balance

Notes: _____

_____

_____

No.	Date	Description	Debit(-)		Credit(+)		Balance

otes: _____

_____

Month / Year:_____ Starting balance:_____

No.	Date	Description	Debit(-)		Credit(+)		Balance

Notes:_____

_____

_____

Month / Year:_____ Starting balance:_____

No.	Date	Description	Debit(-)		Credit(+)		Balance

Notes:_____

_____

Month / Year:_____ Starting balance:_____

No.	Date	Description	Debit(-)		Credit(+)		Balance

Notes:_____

_____

_____

Month / Year:_____ Starting balance:_____

No.	Date	Description	Debit(-)		Credit(+)		Balance

Notes:_____
_____

Month / Year:_____ Starting balance:_____

No.	Date	Description	Debit(-)		Credit(+)		Balance

Notes:_____

_____

_____

onth / Year:_____ Starting balance:_____

No.	Date	Description	Debit(-)		Credit(+)		Balance

otes: _____

_____

Month / Year: _____ Starting balance: _____

No.	Date	Description	Debit(-)		Credit(+)		Balance

Notes: _____

_____

_____

No.	Date	Description	Debit(-)		Credit(+)		Balance

otes:_____

_____

Month / Year:_____ Starting balance:_____

No.	Date	Description	Debit(-)		Credit(+)		Balance

Notes:_____

_____

_____

onth / Year:_____ Starting balance:_____

No.	Date	Description	Debit(-)		Credit(+)		Balance

otes:_____
_____
_____

Month / Year:_____ Starting balance:_____

No.	Date	Description	Debit(-)		Credit(+)		Balance

Notes:_____

_____

_____

onth / Year:_____ Starting balance:_____

No.	Date	Description	Debit(-)		Credit(+)		Balance

otes:_____
_____

Month / Year: _____   Starting balance: _____

No.	Date	Description	Debit(-)		Credit(+)		Balance

Notes: _____

_____

_____

onth / Year:_____ Starting balance:_____

No.	Date	Description	Debit(-)		Credit(+)		Balance

otes:_____
_____

Month / Year:_____ Starting balance:_____

No.	Date	Description	Debit(-)		Credit(+)		Balance

Notes: _____

_____

_____

nth / Year:_____ Starting balance:_____

No.	Date	Description	Debit(-)		Credit(+)		Balance

otes:_____
_____

Month / Year:_____ Starting balance:_____

No.	Date	Description	Debit(-)		Credit(+)		Balance

Notes:_____

_____

_____

onth / Year:_____ Starting balance:_____

No.	Date	Description	Debit(-)		Credit(+)		Balance

otes:_____
_____

Month / Year:_____ Starting balance:_____

No.	Date	Description	Debit(-)		Credit(+)		Balance

Notes:_____

_____

_____

nth / Year: _____			Starting balance: _____			
No.	Date	Description	Debit(-)		Credit(+)		Balance

otes: _____

_____

Month / Year:_____ Starting balance:_____

No.	Date	Description	Debit(-)		Credit(+)		Balance

Notes:_____

_____

_____

Month / Year:_____ Starting balance:_____

No.	Date	Description	Debit(-)		Credit(+)		Balance

Notes:_____

_____

Month / Year:_____   Starting balance:_____

No.	Date	Description	Debit(-)		Credit(+)		Balance

Notes:_____

_____

_____

No.	Date	Description	Debit(-)		Credit(+)		Balance

Notes:_____

_____

Month / Year:_____ Starting balance:_____

No.	Date	Description	Debit(-)		Credit(+)		Balance

Notes:_____

_____

_____

Month / Year:_____ Starting balance:_____

No.	Date	Description	Debit(-)		Credit(+)		Balance

Notes:_____

_____

Month / Year:_____ Starting balance:_____

No.	Date	Description	Debit(-)		Credit(+)		Balance

Notes:_____

_____

_____

_____

onth / Year:_____ Starting balance:_____

No.	Date	Description	Debit(-)		Credit(+)		Balance

otes: _____
_____
_____

Month / Year:_____ Starting balance:_____

No.	Date	Description	Debit(-)		Credit(+)		Balance

Notes:_____

_____

_____

No.	Date	Description	Debit(-)		Credit(+)		Balance

otes:_____
_____
_____

Month / Year: _____ Starting balance: _____

No.	Date	Description	Debit(-)		Credit(+)		Balance

Notes: _____

_____

_____

No.	Date	Description	Debit(-)		Credit(+)		Balance

otes:_____
_____

Month / Year:_____ Starting balance:_____

No.	Date	Description	Debit(-)		Credit(+)		Balance

Notes:_____
_____
_____

No.	Date	Description	Debit(-)		Credit(+)		Balance

otes: _____
_____
_____

Month / Year:_____ Starting balance:_____

No.	Date	Description	Debit(-)		Credit(+)		Balance

Notes:_____
_____
_____

onth / Year: _____ Starting balance: _____

No.	Date	Description	Debit(-)		Credit(+)		Balance

otes: _____

_____

_____

Month / Year:＿＿＿＿＿＿＿＿＿＿＿＿＿ Starting balance:＿＿＿＿＿＿＿＿＿＿

No.	Date	Description	Debit(-)		Credit(+)		Balance

Notes:＿＿＿＿＿＿＿＿＿＿＿＿＿＿＿＿＿＿＿＿＿＿＿＿＿＿＿＿＿＿＿＿＿

＿＿＿＿＿＿＿＿＿＿＿＿＿＿＿＿＿＿＿＿＿＿＿＿＿＿＿＿＿＿＿＿＿＿＿＿

＿＿＿＿＿＿＿＿＿＿＿＿＿＿＿＿＿＿＿＿＿＿＿＿＿＿＿＿＿＿＿＿＿＿＿＿

Month / Year:_____ Starting balance:_____

No.	Date	Description	Debit(-)		Credit(+)		Balance

Notes: _____

_____

Month / Year: _____ Starting balance: _____

No.	Date	Description	Debit(-)		Credit(+)		Balance

Notes: _____

_____

_____

onth / Year:_____ Starting balance:_____

No.	Date	Description	Debit(-)		Credit(+)		Balance

otes:_____
_____

Month / Year:_____ Starting balance:_____

No.	Date	Description	Debit(-)		Credit(+)		Balance

Notes:_____

_____

_____

No.	Date	Description	Debit(-)		Credit(+)		Balance

otes: _____
_____
_____

Month / Year:_____ Starting balance:_____

No.	Date	Description	Debit(-)		Credit(+)		Balance

Notes:_____

_____

_____

No.	Date	Description	Debit(-)		Credit(+)		Balance

otes:_____

_____

Month / Year:_____ Starting balance:_____

No.	Date	Description	Debit(-)		Credit(+)		Balance

Notes:_____

_____

_____

Made in the USA
Las Vegas, NV
07 September 2023

77209481R00063